heart{less}

Marlena Brown

BookLeaf Publishing

Presentation by *BookLeaf Publishing*

Web: www.bookleafpub.com

E-mail: info@bookleafpub.com

ISBN: 9789357695992

First edition 2023

DEDICATION

This is dedicated to all those out there like me, whose path has never been easy. If you're reading this now, you know there's truth to the old saying, get knocked down seven times, rise up eight. Keep rising. Even when it hurts.

ACKNOWLEDGEMENT

Maybe this is where I should acknowledge those who have helped me along the way, but I tend to think about things differently. I'd like to acknowledge all those who were the fabric of my writing. I may not have killed you off in a novel, but I did purge some pretty negative feelings. Things most definitely didn't go as I'd imagined they would, but I'm still standing, and that's something worth acknowledging too.

A Better Man

A marriage can end with a letter
That says we drew a bad hand
Guess there was more worse than there was better
But I thought you were a better man

You compared us to a game of cards
I didn't know you had more up your sleeve
Did I mention about all the cheating
And the lies that I blindly believed
But I thought you were a better man

Right up until I knew that I would leave

I learned that you can't control choices
You can't make someone happy who's not
You can't fix what remains broken
With the hurt and the pain that I've got
When I think back to times I was happy
There's memories but so few with a smile
I wonder what happiness feels like
God knows it's been a long while
But I quit you like a job that was over
Two weeks notice was all I could give
New address I didn't ask for
The cost of the life you wanted to live
And I thought you were a better man

But your promises only got broken
And that letter, just a parting gift
To solidify all I was to you, only a token
And I wanted you to be a better man

But when you play at love like a game
Someone has to lose,
So you win, and I'll fold
All the cards are there on the table
Along with my heart broken and cold
And just like your letter
And your tacky goodbye
And the end of our marriage
And your mouth full of lies
I'll move forward because I can
Finally knowing
You will never be a better man

How Many Times

I wonder how many times
I've hidden in darkness
Shutting out the light
Crying tears in silence
When nothing here is right
How many times I've willed
The dam not to break
Because there was no more room inside my heart
And all the pieces broken for your sake
How many times alone in the shower
With tears rolling down my cheeks
Mixing in with the water beating down
I could stay in here for weeks
How many times I've said I'm fine
When nothing is further from the truth
Wondering how much one person can take
How much more of this I'll go through
How many times I've prayed to God
And wondered if He even hears
Wearing my heart inside out
And drowned by all my tears
How many times I wanted to die
But worried for those left behind
Yet being away from all this pain
Seems better most days in my mind
How many times I've wanted to scream about all the things I feel
But screaming only makes me tired

And my soul is worn out, wonder if it'll ever heal
How many times I've stared out
Into a lake colored vividly blue
How many times I've wondered if I could walk into those waters
And wash myself away, into something new
How many times I've cried myself to sleep at night,
Defeated by the day
How many times I've thought that my life feels pointless
A bad joke too often replayed
How many times I've asked not for easy,
But just for some peace in my soul
And how many times the answer is silence and I'm still here
Cloaked in the darkness, alone

One of These Days

Just a shadow
Just a memory
Of the way I used to be
Just a glimpse in the mirror
I wonder how this can be me
I used to be so different
Only it was a lifetime ago
But I don't remember what that's like
I wonder if I'll ever know
Every single morning
Starts with a silent scream
Feeling like I've failed at life
Can't I wake from this bad dream
Someone I tried to save
That voice is always in my head
Bouncing back and forth inside
Filling me with dread
I wonder why I can't just know
The right words I need to say
Or why I can't just wade through
The suffocating feelings
Drowning me each day
Maybe I will never know
Maybe it's just not meant for me
Maybe it's the penance
I must pay to be be free

Debt

I wanted always to live to serve others
It once brought me joy
Even on days that were sad
But it feels more and more often
That the days just don't ever get better
And joy has been replaced nothing but bad
I never expected life to be easy
I never expected more than my share
But life just keeps beating me down
It's hard now even to care
I can't take more empty promises
If you don't mean the words that you say
Let's not pretend that it matters
Because it doesn't at the end of the day
I wonder if there's a way out of this for me
They say God has a plan for us all
But I'm drowning under waves of weariness
And loneliness hits like a wall
Punched in the gut by these memories
Drawing me in just to push me away
You use love up while you only take
Left with a debt you owe, but one that I must pay

Haunted

In my darkest moments
There's one memory
That won't stay buried
No matter how deep I dig the hole
It's there in that night
When we were still married
When you broke my very soul

You had turned away from me
Laying on your side at the farthest edge
There was no talking, no comfort
Your silence the ear-splitting wedge
That lay between you and me
And I lay there in the dark
Praying my nightly plea
Drowning in loneliness
But you would not save me
Wondering how we could fix this
Afraid, knowing we couldn't
After the tears and the begging
Because you didn't want to
You just wouldn't

But in the darkness
As I'd finally drifted off to sleep
I felt you reach for me
Your hands searching

And my heart skipped a beat
Thinking just maybe
Somehow you'd changed your mind
And when your lips met my lips
And our fingers intertwined
I remember laying so still
Afraid to make a move
Just savoring the way this feels
Because it had been so long
Since I'd felt your touch
I knew I'd missed you terribly
And this reminded me just how much

But then you paused
And you pulled away
Like it never happened at all
I wanted to die
I couldn't believe this
I curled up into a ball
And I cried
And I knew
You'd dreamed of her
You never considered
The way we were
That even in your sleep
It wasn't me you wanted
The shame that night
Left me haunted

I lay there in the dark that night
Staring up at the ceiling
Knowing it'd never again be right

That there would never be healing
Your disappointment, your disdain
Ripped me apart
You'd made it plain
You left barely a shell
All this pain,
All this hell
I will never be the same

And it's been years
But that memory's still there
Doesn't matter
The loneliness, the tears
Or the pain I've had to bear
Some things just don't mend
A soul once hollowed and empty
Creates a rule I just can't bend
Never trusting
Always alone
Haunted by this memory
Just a pile of bones

Crawl

Most days I crawl inside myself
To shut out the hateful words
To block out the world
To shut out the noise
To avoid the words that hurt
The words that say
I'm never enough
That always I will fall short
The words that say
What I should've done
I'm sure you'll share your report
You've always got your reminders
For what I should say or do
You've always got your checklist
To chart ways
I have failed you
So I crawl inside myself
To shut out the wasted words
Trying to escape the way I feel
To block out the world
To shut out the noise
To avoid the words I've already heard
To find solace in silence
From inside this invisible cage
To fly away on the wings of a bird
To a place that is filled with quiet
No hateful words left to read on this page

Lost Soul

Life always seems so hard
And I'm supposed to say I'm fine
I'm supposed to smile
But never define
The stress and the pain
That never seems to leave
If people knew how difficult things are
They'd never believe
You're always tired
I am reminded daily
Someone my age should do better
Yet I'm failing
I'm going to work
I'm doing things day to day
But I want to disappear
More than I have words to say
I feel like I'm too emotional
I'm really just a mess
I'm trying hard to keep it together
Yet it's never enough, not even my best
Collapsing from the outside in
The facade I've built
Can't hold me all in
And it can't hold me together
Foundation is cracked
I'm coming apart at the seams
I guess there's something I've lacked
Maybe it's the love

You never reciprocated
Maybe it's my own stupidity
I couldn't ever have anticipated
Couldn't have seen it coming
Wish I would've known
Wish I could've watched for
The ruining of my soul

Lost

I'm lost
I'm a million grains of sand
Battered b the waves of life
I reach out, but there's no hand
Just washed away
Back out to sea
Nobody to notice
Just let me be

I'm cold
To the bone, deep in my soul
Nothing left to feel in my heart
Just an empty black hole
But the space there just grows
It expands night and day
My existence barely flows
A nebulous disaster, I am light years away

I'm a desert
Barren and alone
Sinking down into the sand
Every breath in me is gone
Loneliness floods the paths to my soul
Sinking again
To the deepest of lows

I'm a soldier
I stumble on, the battle never won
Looking for answers, but still I find none
There is no fight left in me
I hold here the white flag
I just want to surrender,
But i know I'll never be free

I'm I'm still lost

Heart of Stone

Standing int he rain
Water beats down on my head
Rivulets stream down my cheeks
Mixing with my tears and the dread
Of going inside
To my empty house
My empty bed
Of having no place to hide
From these memories
They rear their ugly heads
And then the heartache and pain collide
But it has to be this way
It's how I stay safe
From the way you made me feel
I can't even look me in the face
I wouldn't recognize me anyway
The hollowness behind my eyes
The words I still can't say
The pain I feel
It hurts to breathe
I wish it would stop
That you'd set me free
But I'm a prisoner of
The time and tears
Of the bars I built
To keep out my fears
I failed at love

I've failed at life too
I can't even win at
Forgetting you
I lay in bed with my pillows stacked
In the place you'd lay
A tiny comfort at my back
But I can't make your arms
Reach for me
Help me make it through the day
Hold me
And I can't hear your words
Tell me it'll all be okay
If only
Just for a little while
And I'll fall asleep
Drowning in self pity
Lying in a heap
Of misery and should-have-beens
And promises you didn't keep
And here I am
Heart of stone
And wondering how to do this life
Alone

Heartless

How do I love anyone
Ever again
When love is a weapon
You treat like a sin
Coldness and loneliness
Its only two friends
And how do I love anyone
Ever again

How do I feel love
When my heart's inside out
When it's torn
And I'm bitter
It's been tossed all about
When lies are a constant
And pain is within and without
How do I feel love
When my heart's inside out

And when time has passed
And I look out there for more
I wonder if love is worth waiting for
Or if I'll forever have missed
This empty space in my chest
Where once love could live
But now, I'm left heartless

Invisible

You made me feel invisible
You made me feel alone
You made everything
In life my fault
You made me feel so wrong
Even when I tried to help
Or change to fit your mold
You made it about what I didn't do
You made me feel so cold
You broke my heart
Split it wide open
Did you ever care at all
When your mouth held only lies
I've wondered how things
Could shift so fast
How what I once knew
Was never meant to last
How someone who said
His word was his bond
Could drop lies so quickly
And then he was gone
You made me feel invisible
I was so slow to catch on
To see you for what you were
To accept that I was wrong
To let go of what I thought
Would be life for years to come
Instead you left me behind
With all these tears, just numb

Hollow

I gave all I had in me
You took it all
Won't set me free
And asked for more
Than I could give
But I'd give my all
So you could live
I turned inside out
My heart lay bleeding
Broken pieces full of doubt
Now I'm
Just a hollow shell
I ran through fire
Burned by your hell
Flames found the dust
I'd left behind
Dried in my tears
Consumed by your lies
Just a remnant now
And barely breathing
In the corner
Tired of feeling
Hollow now
From the inside out
A husk, a shell

There is no doubt
I don't know how
Or if
Or when
I'll ever be myself again

Fading

Fading light
My eyes close fast
Embrace the darkness
Can't let this last
The feelings refuse
To dissipate
Wonder how much more of this
That I can take
I want to drift away alone
To collapse in silence
Until the pain is gone
Fading away
Away from light
This life I've lived
Just one long night

Collection

Love is a collection
Of pieces tucked away
Behind all the years
Under words you didn't say
Love is a collection
Behind longed for wishes
Behind countless tears
Under moments of misses
Love is a collection
Of glances not meant for me
Of hurt feelings and pain
When you never said sorry
Because you didn't mean it
And you didn't want to lie
Love is just the beginning
Of the way you said goodbye
Love is a collection
You glance at now and then
A collection of pain and memories
And all the could-have-beens

Missing

I've missed the me I used to be
Have you seen this girl around
I've looked for her for quite some time
But she is missing, can't be found
She used to be the life of the party
But lately that life seems dead
Maybe she's mixed up or lost or confused
Or maybe it's what they've said
That her heart got broken
One time too many
Her give a damn is broken too
That her love for wine is uncanny
Just ask her; she'll tell you
The butt of her own jokes
With laughter that's hollow
Her situation in life
A little hard to swallow
but you might find her dealing
As best as she can
While her give a damn's broken
And her heart's on the mend

Red Lipstick

Tonight I'm going out
Red lipstick, perfect pout
Playlist up
Leaving no doubt
I'm going to have a good time
Because tonight I'm going out

It's been too long
But they're playing my song
Cold beer in hand
Cover band can't get it wrong
It' been too long
But they're playing my song

The music sweeps
Across the room
My heart beats in time
With the drum
I can't remember the last time
I felt like this
A little more alive
A little less numb

Favorite Song

Sitting at the bar
Been forever since I came here
Drink in hand, peeling the label
Like I always do
When I'm thinking
Wondering if I'll ever find someone new
I see you across the room
I watch your finger swirl the rim
Of your whiskey glass
My mind takes a detour
I wonder if you're him
Thinking, don't know how much time has passed
I catch myself imagining your hands on me
It's been so long since I've not felt lonely
Since I shivered with the feel of hot breath
On my neck
I close my eyes
Knowing my life is a wreck
I've considered this too long
Missed seeing you get up to go
And I sigh because now you're gone
And time ticks by so slow
But then here you are
When you lean in close
I smell the whiskey on your breath
And I savor its ghost
I turn to look you in the eyes
My boldness lost quickly

My cheeks burn embarrassed
Like you might've read my mind
And your hand guides me
Out of my chair
When I stand I can't help but lean into you
Like we are the only ones there
It's a heady mix of my thoughts
And where they might lead
And your presence
The smell of whiskey and your cologne
Is mesmerizing
I did not miss the smile
Just at the edge of your lips
Or the way your hands have moved
One sitting just at my hip
As we sway to the music
I know that you're smelling my hair
And you're holding me close
And I'm trying not to stare
The music ends
But I feel like I might drown
If you turn me loose now
I can't just go sit down
But you hold me there on the dance floor
And another song comes on
We sway to the music
And I'm thinking how this is my
New favorite song

Rebirth

I watch the waves
The ebb and the flow
The rhythm, the movement
The pace is so slow
Matches my breathing
The in and the out
The moment is mine
No time here to doubt
I'm alone on this beach
Not a moment too soon
Walking with shadows
And only the moon
Shining down from above
I see its full face
My friend on this night
Glows with its grace
The ocean is calling
Reminds me to breathe
Telling me alone
Can be a gentle reprieve
Alone can mean finding
the broken pieces of me
And building them back
A new version, you see
I'm stronger
I'm better
I'm calmer
I'm wiser

No longer beat down
By cheaters and liears
I bank on my value
I know my own worth
The old me has died
You've seen my rebirth
The moon is my witness
The shadows converge
To share this night with the ocean
With me, and the earth
Reminding me often
The moon, my dear friend
That alone can be beautiful
And my heart now can mend

Moth

I've been hurt and alone,
I've been lied to and burned
But I wrapped myself up
Protected until my rebirth

And into my chrysalis shell
I was folded
Awaiting my new wings
To be dried and unfolded
I won't be a butterfly
Those are made for the light,
No I'll be a moth
I'm a creature of the night
Too much darkness and shadows
Have chased me around
So it's the comfort of darkness
Where I can be found
The moon shines down on me
With her grace and her light
For the creature I am now
A moth of the night

Gently flying
No map of my path to get there
I won't be perfect
With these new wings
That I wear
But I'm flying and free

A moth in the night
Flying toward the moon
And her gentle light

I'm free from the hateful words
And the stress
I'll fly free to the moon
Cloaked in her light as my dress
And my wings help me fly
I'm beautiful once more
I'm a moth of the night
I couldn't ask for more

Three Loves

There are three loves in life, so they say
One that teaches you what love is
But it's not meant to last,
And so it won't stay
The second love is true
And leaves you to heal
So you know what love is,
And what it isn't
And you know when it's real
But the third love is the one that puts
All the pieces into place
It's the one that heals your heart,
The one to offer grace
The one that reminds you
What happiness can be
It's the one that lets you know
The cost of suffering wasn't free
But maybe it was worth it in the end
The third love lets your heart live again

www.ingramcontent.com/pod-product-compliance
Lightning Source LLC
Chambersburg PA
CBHW062204160726
48282CB00027B/989
* 9 7 8 9 3 5 7 6 9 5 9 9 2 *